Broken to Build

Bible Study Curriculum

Crystal Love

Edited by
Nicole Queen

Contents

Introduction

This curriculum invites you to take an introspective look at your life, surrender it completely to God, and arrive at a transformative cross-roads where you can choose a new path forward. Over the next eight weeks, you will embark on a journey toward healing and wholeness. This is a season where God desires to free you from anything that has held you back—whether for years or even your entire life.

The *Broken to Build* Bible Study Curriculum sets the tone for an engaging and transformative experience, exploring the themes of brokenness and renewal. Each week's structure is thoughtfully designed, featuring scripture readings, key themes, and discussion questions to guide participants through a meaningful process of reflection and growth. By sharing personal stories and experiences, participants will have the opportunity to connect the lessons to their own lives, strengthening their trust in God's power and guidance.

Some of the challenges addressed may trace back to events that occurred before you were even born, but God wants to heal the root causes and bring you into a place of complete restoration. As you begin this journey, prepare your heart, embrace the process, and rest in God's promise to make you whole.

Week 1

Don't Forget About Me

"He went to Nazareth, where he had been brought up, and on the Sabbath day, he went into the synagogue, as was his custom. He stood up to read, and the scroll of the prophet Isaiah was handed to him. Unrolling it, he found the place where it is written: 'The Spirit of the Lord is on me, because he has anointed me to proclaim good news to the poor. He has sent me to proclaim freedom for the prisoners and recovery of sight for the blind, to set the oppressed free, to proclaim the year of the Lord's favor.'"

— Luke 4:16-19 (NIV)

Theme:

It is important to acknowledge and address past traumas that have gone unaddressed, allowing the Holy Spirit to guide us in healing and restoration.

Introduction:

The phrase "Don't forget about me" is often associated with a sense of self-centeredness, but in this context, it's a call to acknowledge and address the past traumas that have gone unaddressed.

Biblical Story (Genesis 37-50):

Joseph was sold into slavery by his brothers, who were jealous of his father's favoritism towards him. He was mistreated and forgotten by his Egyptian master, but eventually rose to become a high-ranking official in Egypt. When his brothers came to Egypt seeking food during a famine, Joseph could have easily sought revenge against them for their past wrongdoings. However, instead of holding onto anger and resentment, he chose to forgive them and reconcile with them, saying, "You intended to harm me, but God intended it for good" (Genesis 50:20).

This story shows that even in the face of great trauma and betrayal, we can choose to forgive and move forward, trusting that God can bring good out of our suffering.

Personal Story:

After being emotionally abused in her marriage, Kim struggled to trust and love again, not just with men but in all of her relationships. She felt like she was living in constant fear, never knowing when someone would hurt her again. As she began to share her story with trusted friends and a therapist, Kim started to feel the weight of her trauma lifting. She realized that she didn't have to carry the burden of her wounded past alone, and that God was there to comfort and heal her. With much support and time, Kim began to rebuild her confidence through the Word of God. She understood that the only way to be vulnerable with others was to be vulnerable with God. She realized that forgetting about the past and moving on without healing isn't healthy; neither will it solve the problem.

Just like Kim, some of us run instead of facing the issues at hand. You will not face it alone; God is with you in it all.

* * *

Discussion Questions:

1. What are some past traumas or experiences that you have neglected or suppressed?

_____
_____
_____
_____
_____
_____
_____
_____
_____
_____
_____
_____

2. How have these experiences affected your life and relationships?

_____
_____
_____
_____
_____
_____
_____
_____
_____
_____
_____
_____

3. What does it mean to "not forget about" these past traumas and allow God to heal?

_____

_____

_____

_____

_____

_____

_____

_____

_____

_____

Application:

Take time to reflect on how your actions have impacted your past and current relationships. Write down how you think God wants you to respond to your relationships moving forward.

_____

_____

_____

_____

_____

_____

_____

_____

_____

_____

_____

_____

_____

Reflection:

Reflect on your prayer and application exercise. What do you think God is saying to you about the past traumas or experiences that you have neglected or suppressed? How do you think acknowledging and addressing these experiences can help you move forward in purpose?

_____

_____

_____

_____

_____

_____

_____

_____

_____

_____

_____

_____

_____

_____

_____

_____

Prayer:

Dear God, I acknowledge my past traumas and experiences. Help me to confront them and bring healing and restoration to my life (Psalm 34:18). Give me the courage to forgive and move forward (Colossians 3:13). Be with me as I journey through healing and as you bring good out of my suffering (Romans 8:28). Be my rock, comfort, and strength (Psalm 71:3), and help me trust in your goodness and love, even in the midst of pain and struggle (1 Corinthians 13:7). Give me wisdom and courage to share my story with others so that I can help others who are also struggling (2 Corinthians 1:4).

In Jesus' Name, I pray. Amen.

Memory Verse:

"The Spirit of the Lord is on me,
　　because he has anointed me
　　to proclaim good news to the poor.
　　He has sent me to proclaim freedom for the prisoners
　　and recovery of sight for the blind,
　　to set the oppressed free,
　　to proclaim the year of the Lord's favor."

— Luke 4:18-19

* * *

Take some time to journal about a moment in your life when you intentionally dismissed your feelings and chose to move on, even though the situation was too painful to address. How did you respond? What were your thoughts and emotions?

Pray and ask God to reveal whether you have developed a habit of avoidance as a way to numb the pain. Write down what you heard from God and any promises He gave you. Then, find a scripture from both the Old Testament and the New Testament that correlates with your responses.

Share your struggles and breakthroughs with a small group of believers or an accountability partner. Ask them to pray for you and encourage you as you work through breaking down strongholds in your life.

_____

_____

_____

_____

_____

_____

Week 2

The Broken System

"The Lord is compassionate and gracious, slow to anger, abounding in love. He will not always accuse, nor will he harbor his anger forever; He does not treat us as our sins deserve or repay us according to our iniquities. For as high as the heavens are above the earth, so great is his love for those who fear him; as far as the east is from the west, so far has he removed our transgressions from us. As a father has compassion on his children, so the Lord has compassion on those who fear him; for he knows how we are formed, he remembers that we are dust."

— Psalm 103:8-14 (NLT)

Since ancient times no one has heard, no ear has perceived, no eye has seen any God besides you, who acts on behalf of those who wait for him.

— Isaiah 64:4 (NIV)

Theme:

There are limitations in our own strength and abilities, but in Christ and the Kingdom of God, we can accomplish more. We have the advantage over the systems of this world.

Introduction:

As we navigate the complexities of life, we often find ourselves trying to fix our own problems and situations, relying on our own strength and abilities to overcome challenges. However, when we attempt to fix problems or situations, it often leads to frustration and failure. God is breaking down our old faulty system and recalibrating everything in our lives to create a new way of living, according to His word, rather than the system of this world.

Biblical Story (Genesis 28:10-22):

The story of Jacob is a powerful example of acknowledging our limitations and trusting in God's power. After running from his brother Esau, Jacob stopped to rest and fell asleep, having a dream in which he saw angels ascending and descending. In this dream, Jacob saw and experienced God's presence. He heard God's promise to bless him and make him a great nation. When Jacob woke up, he realized that he was in the presence of God and didn't even know it. He knew that this promise could not be achieved in his own strength. He became overwhelmed, like many of us; however, he was willing to go through this process to walk out what God promised as long as he knew that God was with him.

Personal Story:

After being diagnosed with illness after illness, Marsha felt like her life was turned upside down. She struggled with the temporary reality that this may be it, time after time. She wondered if she had done something wrong. Maybe it was her consistently searching for acceptance and fulfillment in relationships when all the while it was never enough. She still found herself unhealed, broken, and empty.

Broken promises lead to brokenness in mind, heart, and soul, and in her case, her body. She didn't realize that she was putting her body through much trauma by holding all of the disappointments inside.

Until one day, Marsha began to realize, "I have to release the pain so that I can receive my healing."

Healing is never a superficial thing; it is a real experience for a real change. This is something that only God can do. Marsha realized that her pain was an opportunity for God to show up and get all of the glory from her testimony. She learned that after the process of healing inside and out, God was there with her the entire time. She found peace in the suffering and victory in her healing. Isaiah 61:3 reminds us of beauty for ashes, the oil of joy for mourning, and the garment of praise for the spirit of heaviness.

* * *

Discussion Questions:

1. What are some ways you may try to fix your own problems or situations? (Psalm 103:8-14)

_____
_____
_____
_____
_____
_____
_____
_____
_____
_____
_____
_____
_____
_____
_____
_____

2. How do you tend to rely on your own strength and abilities?
(Isaiah 64:4)

_____

_____

_____

_____

_____

_____

_____

_____

_____

_____

_____

_____

_____

_____

3. What does it mean to acknowledge that you are broken and in
need of God's help?

_____

_____

_____

_____

_____

_____

_____

_____

_____

_____

_____

_____

_____

Application:

Write down a time when you tried to fix a problem or situation on your own. What was the outcome?

_____

_____

_____

_____

_____

_____

_____

_____

_____

_____

_____

Reflection:

Reflect on how you can learn to trust in God's power and guidance instead of relying on your own strength.

_____

_____

_____

_____

_____

_____

_____

_____

_____

_____

_____

Prayer:

Dear God, I acknowledge that I am not self-sufficient, but rather in need of your guidance and power. I confess that I often try to fix my own problems and situations, relying on my own strength and abilities, but I know that this can lead to frustration and failure. Help me to trust in your goodness and love, as you have promised to be slow to anger and abounding in love (Psalm 103:8-14). Remind me that you are the one who acts on behalf of those who wait for you and that you have removed my transgressions from me as far as the east is from the west (Isaiah 64:4). May I learn to acknowledge my brokenness and dependence on you, and may I trust in your power to guide me through the complexities of life. Help me to see that even in the darkest moments, you are still present and still in control.

In Jesus' Name, I pray. Amen.

Memory Verse:

Since ancient times no one has heard,
    no ear has perceived,
    no eye has seen any God besides you,
    who acts on behalf of those who wait for him.

— Isaiah 64:4 NIV

* * *

Take some time to journal on a time in your life where the people around you, from your perspective, did not understand what was going on within. How did you respond? What were your thoughts and emotions?

Pray and ask God to reveal to you if the people around you were the problem and if you should embrace new connections and invest more time in working on those that are fruitful. Write about what you heard from God and any promises He gave you. Find a scripture from the Old Testament and New Testament to correlate with your responses.

Share your struggles and breakthroughs with a small group of believers or an accountability partner. Ask them to pray for you and encourage you as you work through breaking down strongholds in your life.

_____

_____

_____

_____

_____

_____

_____

_____

_____

_____

_____

_____

_____

_____

_____

_____

_____

_____

_____

_____

_____

_____

_____

_____

_____

_____

Week 3

Bound to Break

"Before I was afflicted, I went astray: but now have I kept thy word. Thou art good, and doth good; Praise be to the Lord forever: I will keep thy statutes forever. The proud have forged a lie against me: but I will keep thy precepts with my whole heart. Their heart is as fat as butter; but I will take heed to thy commandments. It is good for me that I have been afflicted; that I may learn thy statutes.

— Psalm 119:67-71 (KJV)

Jesus, when he had received the vinegar, said, "It is finished." And he bowed his head and gave up his spirit.

—John 19:30 (KJV)

Theme:

Recognizing and responding to warning signs that indicate we are approaching a breaking point is essential; we must continue to trust in God's healing power in our brokenness.

Introduction:

The concept of reaching a breaking point in life can sound troubling at first thought. This lesson highlights how people often struggle to cope with their emotions and challenges, and how Jesus shows compassion and understanding to those who are struggling.

We will explore the importance of recognizing and responding to warning signs that indicate we're approaching a breaking point and learning to trust in God's healing power in our brokenness.

Biblical Story (John 4:4-42):

The story of the Samaritan Woman at the well is a powerful example of vulnerability and change. Jesus meets a woman who has been ostracized by her community because of her past and present situation. Coming to the well alone could have been her way of escaping being the talk of the town because of her relationships with the men she looked to for comfort. Jesus shows up, letting her know that the well she needs to drink from will yield what she's been looking for all along: this is a gift freely given that would elevate all of the fears and disappointments of her past and current situation. She received the living water of forgiveness and spiritual awakening. Her life with Christ had begun, and she couldn't wait to share her experience with a man, the Savior of the world, who knew everything about her and did not judge but healed her.

When we are in our darkest times, life can feel like we can't recover from our mistakes. God sees it and knows it, and He is coming with a resolution and healing. He will judge righteously, for there is therefore no condemnation for those who are in Christ Jesus.

Personal Story:

Veronica struggled with coming to terms with the fact that she was different. Of course, many of us know that we all have many traits about us that can't be compared to others, but we often find ourselves striving to do and be like other people, especially when we're not satisfied with ourselves. Veronica was quiet and timid and was not as outgoing as the people around her, which caused her to feel secluded and develop low self-esteem. Being raised in church, marriage, children, and still feeling the void of not feeling like she was enough caused her to go out into the world and experience things that she would never have imagined she would do: addiction, near-death experiences, abuse, pain, and neglect. She finally rededicated her life back to Christ and was restored to her rightful place.

We will realize in our life journey that all the while we're trying to find who we are, we cannot figure that out without God because He wrote our entire life script, and all we have to do is follow and live by what He has already planned out for us.

* * *

Discussion Questions:

1. Name some particular areas in your life that need to break off of you in order for you to progress in your future endeavors.

_____

_____

_____

_____

_____

_____

_____

_____

_____

_____

_____

2. What are some signs that indicate that you may be on the verge of a breaking point? (John 19:30)

_____

_____

_____

_____

_____

_____

_____

_____

_____

_____

_____

_____

_____

3. How can you learn to recognize and respond to these warning signs?

_____

_____

_____

_____

_____

_____

_____

_____

_____

_____

_____

_____

_____

_____

Application:

Reflect on past experiences of breaking points. Write down what God is trying to say about them. Acknowledge and address them with God's guidance.

_____
_____
_____
_____
_____
_____
_____
_____
_____
_____
_____
_____

Reflection:

Reflect on how you often put yourself in situations where you are bound to break. What happened? How did you respond?

_____
_____
_____
_____
_____
_____
_____
_____
_____
_____
_____
_____

Prayer:

Dear God, we acknowledge that we are fragile and prone to breaking, and that we often put ourselves in situations where we are bound to break. We confess that we may not always recognize the warning signs that indicate we are approaching a breaking point, but we know that you are always present and willing to listen. Help us to trust in your healing power in our brokenness, and may we find liberation and new life in our openness. Remind us that it is good for us to be afflicted, that we may learn your ways (Psalm 119:71). May we find strength in your goodness and love, even in the darkest moments.

In Jesus' Name, I pray. Amen.

Memory Verse:

It is good for me that I have been afflicted;
   that I may learn thy statutes.

— Psalms 119:71

* * *

Take some time to journal on a time in your life where you felt that you were almost at your breaking point. How did you respond? What were your thoughts and emotions?

Pray and ask God to reveal what stopped you. Write about what you heard from God and any promises He gave you.

Share your struggles and breakthroughs with a small group of believers or an accountability partner. Ask them to pray for you and encourage you as you work through breaking down strongholds in your life.

Week 4

When I Broke, I Healed

I will extol the Lord at all times; his praise will always be on my lips. I will glory in the Lord; let everyone on earth glorify his holy name. Declare his glory among the nations, his marvelous deeds among all peoples. For great is the Lord above all gods, the Lord Almighty, beyond all praise. Who is like you, Lord God Almighty? You, Lord, are mighty, and your faithfulness surrounds you.

— Psalm 30:1-5 (NIV)

But he was pierced for our transgressions, he was crushed for our iniquities; the punishment that brought us peace was on him, and by his wounds we are healed.

— Isaiah 53:5 (NIV)

Theme:

When we break, we can discover that God's healing power is strongest in our brokenness.

Introduction:

Have you ever felt like you're at your breaking point? Like the stress, anxiety, and overwhelm are too much to bear? Maybe you've experienced a 'broken' moment in your life—a moment when everything fell apart and you felt like you couldn't put the pieces back together.

In this lesson, we're going to explore what happens when we break and how we can find healing and restoration in the midst of our brokenness.

Biblical Story (Job 1-42):

Job's story is one of brokenness and healing. He was a righteous man who suffered greatly, losing his family, his health, and his possessions. As we look at this story, many of us can say that we have faced or are facing a Job-like experience; in many ways, we can identify with the one thing after another that Job experienced, along with the opinions of his friends and, most importantly, his dedication and relationship with God.

Despite all that he endured, he never turned his back on God. Yes, he was angry and felt lost, but at the same time, he knew that God was with him and that he would be okay. God used this brokenness to bring Job closer to Himself and to go through the refining process because a double portion was getting ready to come his way.

In Job 42:5-6, Job says, "I have heard of thee by the hearing of the ear: but now mine eye seeth thee... Wherefore I abhor myself, and repent in dust and ashes."

Job's story reminds us that we are not alone, no matter who is in our ear—family, friends, or even ourselves—that God is working it out for our good, and healing and restoration are taking place.

Personal Story:

A single dad with four children answered the call of God while facing many adversities in his life: loss of a job, his wife, and many friends who decided to walk away from him. Holding the office as a prophet of God, willingly accepting this call brought much brokenness into his life, but John realized that his life was totally dedicated to God. What mattered the most was that he would be an example to his children, as well as to those he was teaching and preaching to. His family experienced many transitions because of his call in the Body of Christ, but all the while, it was grooming them for what they were going to become in the Kingdom of God.

As parents and mentors, you may not realize the impact of your 'yes' and what it has on the people who look up to you. Whether he was moving to a new city to build a ministry or traveling locally to preach the gospel, it was his commission to Christ that caused so many to be impacted long after his physical life. His testimony would echo from decade to decade.

Therefore, make your life memorable by following Jesus and leave your imprint in the world; it will be a resounding testimony of bravery and submission to God.

* * *

Discussion Questions:

1. Have you ever experienced a "broken" moment in your life? How did you heal? (Psalm 30:1-5)

_____

_____

_____

_____

_____
_____
_____
_____
_____
_____
_____
_____

2. What are some common ways we try to self-soothe or medicate our emotional pain? (Isaiah 53:5)

_____
_____
_____
_____
_____
_____
_____
_____
_____

3. How can we learn to trust in God's healing power in our brokenness?

_____
_____
_____
_____
_____
_____
_____
_____
_____

Application:

Identify areas in your life where you may be putting yourself in situations where you are prone to breaking (e.g., overcommitting, pushing yourself too hard, etc.). What changes can you make to reduce stress and increase self-care?

_____

_____

_____

_____

_____

_____

_____

_____

_____

_____

Reflection:

Write down some coping mechanisms that you have used in the past when you felt disappointed in your brokenness. Did they work? And would you use them again?

_____

_____

_____

_____

_____

_____

_____

_____

_____

_____

_____

Prayer:

Dear God, I acknowledge that in the weak areas of my life, I am fragile and prone to breaking. I confess that I may not always recognize the warning signs that indicate I am approaching a breaking point, but I know that you are always present and willing to listen. Help me to trust in your healing power in my brokenness, and may I find liberation and new life in my openness. Remind me that it is good for me to be afflicted, that I may learn your ways (Psalm 119:71). May I find strength in your goodness and love, even in the darkest moments.

In Jesus' Name, I pray. Amen.

Memory Verse:

But he was pierced for our transgressions,
    he was crushed for our iniquities;
    the punishment that brought us peace was on him,
    and by his wounds we are healed.

— Isaiah 53:5 (NIV)

* * *

Take some time to journal on a recent situation where you felt that you were not in a safe place to break. What were your thoughts and emotions?

Pray and ask God to reveal the root of why you didn't feel that you could break open and release. Write about what you heard from God and any promises He gave you. Find a Scripture from the Old Testament and the New Testament to correlate with your responses.

Share your struggles and breakthroughs with a small group of believers or an accountability partner. Ask them to pray for you and encourage you as you work through breaking down strongholds in your life.

_____

_____

_____

_____

_____

_____

_____

_____

_____

_____

_____

_____

_____

_____

_____

_____

_____

_____

_____

_____

_____

_____

_____

_____

_____

_____

_____

_____

_____

_____

_____

_____

_____

Week 5

Broken to Build

Have mercy on me, O God, because of your unfailing love.
Because your compassion is always ready, and your conso-
lation knows no fault, Wash away all my iniquity and
cleanse me from my guilt.

For I know that you delight in truth. Not sacrifice, but truth is
what You will. Then I will teach transgressors Your ways,
and sinners will return to you.

Wash me thoroughly and I shall be whiter than snow. Make
me hear joy and gladness, that the bones You have broken
may rejoice. Hide Your face from my sins and blot out all
my iniquities. Create in me a clean heart, O God, and
renew a steadfast spirit within me.

Do not cast me away from Your presence and do not take Your
Holy Spirit from me. Restore to me the joy of Your salva-
tion and sustain me with a willing spirit.

Then I will teach transgressors Your ways, and sinners will
return to you. Do good, O Lord, to those who are good, to
the upright in their hearts.

But as for me, I will walk in my integrity; redeem me and be
merciful to me. My tongue will declare Your righteousness

*and Your salvation all day long; for I do not know how to
curse an enemy or oppress those who are helpless.*
*Surely I have calmed and quieted myself like a weaned child
with his mother; like a weaned child, I am content. When
Israel was a child, I loved him; and I called My son, they
are the children of My loving-kindness.*
*The time has come when they should be dealt with according to
the former loving-kindness. Wash me thoroughly; I shall be
whiter than snow. Make me hear joy and gladness, that the
bones You have broken may rejoice. Hide Your face from
my sins and blot out all my iniquities.*

— Psalm 51:1-17 NIV

*The Spirit of the Sovereign Lord is on me, because the Lord has
anointed me to proclaim good news to the poor. He has sent me to bind
up the brokenhearted, to proclaim freedom for the captives and release
from darkness for the prisoners, to proclaim the year of the Lord's favor
and the day of vengeance of our God, to comfort all who mourn, and
provide for those who grieve in Zion—to bestow on them a crown of
beauty instead of ashes, the oil of joy instead of mourning, and a
garment of praise instead of a spirit of despair. They will be called
oaks of righteousness, a planting of the Lord for the display of his
splendor.*

— Isaiah 61:1-3 NIV

Theme:

Breaking free from limitations allows us to receive revelation and
walk in God's power and authority.

Introduction:

Sometimes, we face problems that seem too big to handle, and we
may feel like we're stuck. But the truth is, God has a plan to fix

everything and bring us closer to Him. In this study, we'll explore how God's power and authority can be accessed by breaking down problems and rebuilding life according to His plan out of our brokenness.

Biblical Story:

The story of Peter's progression from "Simon" to "Peter, son of Jonah" to simply "Peter" (Matthew 16:13-20, John 1:42) shows how he received revelations about who Jesus was and learned to walk in His power and authority. Peter's journey is a powerful reminder that we all need to die to our old selves and follow Jesus to receive the keys to unlock God's power and authority. Many can look at Peter's life and see his passion for Jesus Christ and the things that God had called him to do on the earth. He was a fiery one, and Jesus used it for His glory. He denied Jesus three times because of fear, but he also vowed later to love Jesus and to feed His sheep. Being a bold soldier and preaching the gospel after Jesus left the earth, he caused 3,000 people to give their lives to Christ. It does not matter what we have faced or gone through; all that matters is how we finish. (Acts 2:14-21).

Personal Story:

Anthony took a leap of faith that saved his life. He had to leave the familiar to step into his calling with all diligence and focus. He left the life behind, the street life, to cause others to be delivered. He realized that though his former life was a choice, he also knew that the environment fostered these decisions as well. Quick money and 'the good life' at the cost of almost losing your life are not worth the sacrifice. The Bible says, 'What profit is it to a man to gain the world and lose his soul?' How many of us are willing to leave what appears to be prosperous to walk into the unknown, not knowing what's on the other side? Whatever is in Christ is good. There are no mistakes in choosing Christ; that is the best decision that you could ever make in your life. When Anthony made the decision to leave the world of fast money and illegal transactions that caused other people's downfall, that was the best decision he could ever make. Now he's winning souls for Christ and helping people to walk in their God-given calling.

* * *

Discussion Questions:

1. What is a problem or situation in your life that feels too big to handle?

_____

_____

_____

_____

_____

_____

_____

_____

_____

2. Have you ever experienced a moment of revelation that changed your perspective or understanding of God's plan for your life?

_____

_____

_____

_____

_____

_____

_____

_____

_____

_____

3. How can you apply the principle of breaking down problems and rebuilding them to your current situation?

_____

_____

_____

_____

_____

_____

_____

_____

_____

_____

_____

_____

_____

4. What are some areas in your life where you may need to "die to yourself" and follow Jesus more closely?

_____

_____

_____

_____

_____

_____

_____

_____

_____

_____

_____

_____

_____

_____

Application:

Ask God to reveal His plan for your life and give you the strength to walk in His power and authority. Identify one area in your life where you need to break down a problem or situation and rebuild it according to God's plan. Consider what small steps you can take today to start breaking down the problem or situation and ask God for wisdom and guidance as you rebuild.

_____
_____
_____
_____
_____
_____
_____
_____
_____
_____
_____
_____

Reflection:

Search the Scriptures to find some examples in the Bible, where certain people had to die to themselves. Choose out the main highlighting principles that were used and how you can apply that to your life.

_____
_____
_____
_____
_____
_____
_____

_____
_____
_____
_____
_____
_____
_____
_____
_____
_____
_____
_____

Prayer:

"Dear Lord, I come to You with my problems and worries. Help me to have eyes to see Your plan for my life and the strength to walk in Your power and authority. Give me revelation about areas where I need to allow You to break down and rebuild again according to Your plan. Help me die to myself and follow You more closely. I pray that You would give me wisdom and guidance as I navigate this journey and grant me strength and wisdom as I face spiritual battles. Help me to arm myself with prayer and the spiritual disciplines that draw me closer to You.

In Jesus' name, I pray, Amen."

Memory Verse:

The Spirit of the Sovereign Lord is on me, because the Lord has anointed me to proclaim good news to the poor. He has sent me to bind up the brokenhearted, to proclaim liberty to the captives, and the opening of the prison to those who are bound.

— Isaiah 61:1

* * *

Take some time to journal on a recent situation where you felt stuck or overwhelmed. How did you respond? What were your thoughts and emotions?

Pray and ask God to reveal His plan for your life and give you the strength to walk in His power and authority. Write about what you heard from God and any promises He gave you. Find a scripture from the Old Testament and the New Testament to correlate with your responses.

Share your struggles and breakthroughs with a small group of believers or an accountability partner. Ask them to pray for you and encourage you as you work through breaking down strongholds in your life.

_____

_____

_____

_____

_____

_____

_____

_____

_____

_____

_____

_____

_____

_____

_____

_____

_____

_____

_____

_____

_____

Week 6

Strategies for War

Finally, be strong in the Lord and in his mighty power. Put on the full armor of God, so that you can take your stand against the devil's schemes. For our struggle is not against flesh and blood, but against the rulers, against the authorities, against the powers of this dark world and against the evil forces of the spiritual kingdom of this world against which we wrestle.

Therefore, put on the full armor of God, so that when the day of evil comes, you may be able to stand your ground, and having done everything, to stand. Stand firm then, with your feet fitted with the readiness that comes from the gospel of peace.

In addition to all this, take up the shield of faith, with which you can extinguish all the flaming arrows of the evil one.

Take the helmet of salvation and the sword of the Spirit, which is the word of God.

And pray in the Spirit on all occasions with all kinds of prayers and requests. With this in mind, be alert and always keep on praying for all the Lord's people.

Pray also for me, that whenever I speak, words may be given me so that I will fearlessly make known the mystery of the gospel, for which I am an ambassador in chains. Pray that I may declare it fearlessly, as I should. For I know that through your prayers I will be delivered from decay and that you will be safe.

— Ephesians 6:10-20 (NIV)

Whoever dwells in the shelter of the Most High will rest in the shadow of the Almighty.
I will say of the Lord, "He is my refuge and my fortress, my God, in whom I trust."
Surely he will save you from the fowler's snare and from the deadly pestilence.
He will cover you with his feathers, and under his wings you will find refuge; his faithfulness will be your shield and rampart.
You will not fear the terror of night, nor the arrow that flies by day, nor the pestilence that stalks in the darkness, nor the plague that destroys at midday.
A thousand may fall at your side, ten thousand at your right hand, but it will not come near you.
You will only observe with your eyes and see the punishment of the wicked.
If you say, "The Lord is my refuge," and you make the Most High your dwelling, no harm will overtake you, no disaster will come near your tent.
For he will command his angels concerning you to guard you in all your ways; they will lift you up in their hands, so that you will not strike your foot against a stone.
You will tread on the lion and the cobra; you will trample the great lion and the serpent.

"Because he loves me," says the Lord, "I will rescue him; I
will protect him, for he acknowledges my name.
He will call on me, and I will answer him; I will be with him
in trouble, I will deliver him and honor him. With long
life I will satisfy him and show him my salvation.

— *Psalm 91 (NIV)*

Theme:

God has given us the power to break and destroy strongholds in our lives.

Introduction:

As we begin this Bible study on "Breaking and Destroying Strongholds," we are reminded that the enemy's ultimate goal is to kill, steal, and destroy all that is good in our lives. This can manifest in many ways, from the subtle whispers of doubt and fear to the all-consuming grip of addiction or depression. But the truth is, strongholds are not just external circumstances, but often battles within our own minds and hearts. They are entities that have taken up residence, exerting a powerful influence over our thoughts, emotions, and actions. Perhaps you have felt the weight of a stronghold in your life—a sense of being trapped, controlled, or consumed by forces beyond your control. As we dive into this study, we will explore the strategies for war that God has given us to break free from these strongholds and live a life of freedom and purpose.

Biblical Story:

David and Goliath is an example of breaking and destroying strongholds. David was a young but strong leader who was prepared for Goliath and all the other enemies of Israel that God used him to destroy, being a shepherd boy. Many of us in life despise our past and upbringing, not knowing that it has given us the strength to face every Goliath in our lives. Your past prepared you for your present, and your present is preparing you to pass the baton to somebody else. It was through the lineage of David that Jesus came. He had to be a strong and mighty warrior for God because of what was going to happen through his life. Goliath was intimidating by others, but David looked at him as an uncircumcised Philistine who could not come up against the all-powerful, all-knowing, true and living God that David knew about. David trusted in the power of God, not the fear of man. He heard the call, and he responded in faith and obedience. That is all that God requires us to do: hear Him and respond by action. (1 Samuel 17).

Personal Story:

Jennifer had been in a war in her mind ever since she was a little girl. She could not understand why the battle was so strong, but when she got older and gave her life to Christ, God began to give her a revelation of what was going on. She understood that it went back farther than she thought. She realized that mental illness was in her bloodline, but she was so determined that the fight was going to stop with her.

There are things in life where the battle started long before we got here, and it also continued before we even knew we were in a fight. She thought it was her. She thought there was something wrong with her as to why she could not focus. She didn't understand why it took her so long to grasp concepts and why she had such difficulty pressing through what appeared to be normal to others. She struggled in school; she dealt with depression, anxiety, and fear, which put a strain on her relationships and caused her to doubt who God created her to be. But through much prayer and wise, godly counsel, she was able to break through and receive her deliverance.

It was something that she was determined to achieve, so she would read her Bible, fast, pray, attend prayer gatherings, and, most importantly, say yes to God. She was delivered! By saying yes, she did not let her challenges stop her from fulfilling her purpose in the Kingdom of God.

* * *

Discussion Questions:

1. How do you think strongholds develop in our lives?

_____

_____

_____

_____

_____

_____

_____

_____

_____

_____

2. What are some common tactics used by the enemy to build strongholds?

_____

_____

_____

_____

_____

_____

_____

_____

_____

_____

_____

3. How can we break and destroy strongholds in our lives?

_____

_____

_____

_____

_____

_____

_____

_____

_____

_____

_____

_____

_____

_____

_____

4. What role does discernment play in recognizing and overcoming strongholds?

_____

_____

_____

_____

_____

_____

_____

_____

_____

_____

_____

_____

_____

_____

Application:

Apply the principles of breaking and destroying strongholds to your own life. Identify areas where you need to surrender your old ways and receive new life from God. Practice discernment by seeking God's guidance and wisdom in your decisions.

_____

_____

_____

_____

_____

_____

_____

_____

_____

_____

Reflection:

Reflect on a time when you felt trapped by a stronghold. Think about what you did to break free from that stronghold. Consider what steps you can take today to prevent future strongholds from forming.

_____

_____

_____

_____

_____

_____

_____

_____

_____

_____

Prayer:

Dear Lord, help me to recognize the strongholds that have been building up in my life. Give me the courage and strength to break free from their hold and surrender my old ways. Fill me with your Holy Spirit and guide me toward new life.

In Jesus' name I pray, Amen.

Memory Verse:

We demolish arguments and every pretension that sets itself up against the knowledge of God, and we take captive every thought to make it obedient to Christ.

— 2 Corinthians 10:5 (NIV)

* * *

Take some time to journal on a moment in your life where you intentionally dismissed your feelings and proceeded to move on because the situation was too painful to address. How did you respond? What were your thoughts and emotions?

Pray and ask God to reveal to you whether or not you have developed a habit of avoidance to numb the pain. Write about what you heard from God and any promises He gave you. Find a scripture from the Old Testament and New Testament to correlate with your responses.

Share your struggles and breakthroughs with a small group of believers or an accountability partner. Ask them to pray for you and encourage you as you work through breaking down strongholds in your life.

Week 7

The Induction of the New You

"I am crucified with Christ; nevertheless I live; yet not I, but Christ liveth in me: and the life which I now live in the flesh, I live by the faith of the Son of God, who loved me, and gave himself for me."

— *Galatians 2:20 (KJV)*

"But we all, with open face beholding as in a glass the glory of the Lord, are changed into the same image from glory to glory, even as by the Spirit of the Lord."

— *2 Corinthians 3:18 (KJV)*

"Beloved, now are we the sons of God, and it doth not yet appear what we shall be: but we know that, when he shall appear, we shall be like him; for we shall see him as he is."

— *1 John 3:2 (KJV)*

Theme:

Through induction into faith, transformation by the Holy Spirit, and embracing our identity in Christ, we are empowered to live a life of purpose and fulfillment.

Introduction:

As we journey through this study, we'll explore the theme of induction, which is the process of being transformed into the image of Christ. We'll examine how God's words and actions shape our understanding of ourselves and our identities in Him.

Biblical Story:

The story of Israel's 40 years in the wilderness truly shows how God can, number one, provide, and number two. It also shows us how we can repeat cycles over and over again, sometimes never fully walking in the promises of God. This is one thing that God wants us to take from the story so that we can avoid missing out on what He has purposed us to experience while we are here on earth and do it in His timing.

There are some of us living in regret, and I'm sure that the Israelites began to see the same thing happening over and over again. They understood that the cycle needed to be broken, but oftentimes, because we don't yield to God, we miss seasons and opportunities to soar as God intended. But this is what God wants us to learn so that we can receive everything that He has for us.

Personal Story:

Share your own story of transformation or struggle with identity. How have you experienced the transformation of God in your life? Use the space on the following page to write your personal story.

_____

_____

_____

* * *

Discussion Questions:

1. How do you think your identity is shaped by your experiences and circumstances?

_____
_____
_____
_____
_____
_____
_____
_____
_____
_____
_____
_____

2. In what ways have you seen God transform your life or the lives of those around you?

_____
_____
_____
_____
_____
_____
_____
_____
_____
_____
_____
_____

3. What does it mean to you to be transformed into the image of Christ?

_____

_____

_____

_____

_____

_____

_____

_____

_____

_____

Application:

Choose one of the declarations below and write it out in your own words. Make it personal by replacing "I" with "I am" (e.g., "I am a new creation in Christ"). Repeat this declaration out loud to yourself daily, using the corresponding scripture as a reference. Share your declaration with a friend or accountability partner to help hold each other accountable.

Declarations:

- I am a new creation in Christ (2 Corinthians 5:17).
- I am a child of God (John 1:12).
- I am redeemed and forgiven (Ephesians 1:7).
- I am filled with the Holy Spirit (Acts 2:4).
- I am more than a conqueror (Romans 8:37).

_____

_____

_____

_____

_____

_____
_____
_____
_____
_____
_____
_____
_____
_____
_____
_____
_____
_____
_____

Reflection:

Take some time to reflect on how your past experiences and circumstances have shaped your sense of identity. Consider how God's
words and actions have impacted your understanding of yourself.

_____
_____
_____
_____
_____
_____
_____
_____
_____
_____
_____
_____
_____
_____

Prayer:

Ask God to help you understand and internalize your new identity in Christ. Pray that you would become more like Him as you journey through life together. Utilize Romans 8:37 as the basis for your prayer.

Memory Verse:

> Know ye not that ye are the temple of God, and that the Spirit of God dwelleth in you? If any man defile the temple of God, him shall God destroy; for the temple of God is holy, which temple ye are. Write down three ways you can apply this passage to your life.
>
> — 1 Corinthians 3:16-17 (KJV)

* * *

Write out one specific area where you feel like you're struggling with your identity or sense of self-worth. Ask God to speak to this area and bring transformation to your life.

Find a friend or accountability partner to share your struggles and triumphs with, and ask them to do the same for you. Meet up with each other once a week to pray and encourage one another.

_____
_____
_____
_____
_____
_____
_____
_____
_____
_____

Week 8

Restoration and Refining

"This is what the Lord Almighty says: 'In a little while, I will once more shake the heavens and the earth, the sea, and the dry land. I will shake all nations, and what is desired by all nations will come—and I will fill this house with glory,' says the Lord Almighty. 'The silver is mine and the gold is mine,' declares the Lord Almighty. The glory of this latter house will be greater than the glory of the former; and in this place, I will give peace,' says the Lord Almighty."

— Haggai 2:6-9 (NIV)

"Therefore, if any man be in Christ, he is a new creature: old things are passed away; behold, all things are become new."

— 2 Corinthians 5:17 (KJV)

"Now these are the people of the province who came up from the captivity of the exiles, whom Nebuchadnezzar king of Babylon had taken captive to Babylon (they returned to Jerusalem and Judah, each to their own town, in company with Zerubbabel, Joshua, Nehemiah, Seraiah, Reelaiah, Mordecai, Bilshan, Mispar, Bigvai, Rehum and Baanah): The list of the men of the people of Israel...

And from among the priests: The descendants of Hobaiah, Hakkoz and Barzillai (a man who had married a daughter of Barzillai the Gileadite and was called by that name). These searched for their family records, but they could not find them and so were excluded from the priesthood as unclean. The governor ordered them not to eat any of the most sacred food until there was a priest ministering with the Urim and Thummim.

The whole company numbered 42,360, 65 besides their 7,337 male and female slaves; and they also had 200 male and female singers. They had 736 horses, 245 mules, 67 435 camels and 6,720 donkeys. When they arrived at the house of the Lord in Jerusalem, some of the heads of the families gave freewill offerings toward the rebuilding of the house of God on its site. 69 According to their ability they gave to the treasury for this work 61,000 darics of gold, 5,000 minas of silver and 100 priestly garments. The priests, the Levites, the musicians, the gatekeepers and the temple servants settled in their own towns, along with some of the other people, and the rest of the Israelites settled in their towns."

— *Ezra 2:1-70 (verses 1-2, 61-70 above)*

Theme:

Through the process of restoration and refinement, you can learn how to apply biblical principles to fill your life with God's presence.

Introduction:

In the book of Ezra, we read about the Israelites' return to Jerusalem after the exile. They faced a daunting task: rebuilding the temple and restoring their relationship with God. As we reflect on this story, we're reminded that our own lives are often marked by brokenness and reconstruction. In this lesson, we'll explore the parallels between the natural process of rebuilding and the spiritual process of restoration.

Biblical Stories:

The Israelites

The story of the Israelites' return to Jerusalem from exile is a powerful example of restoration and refining. After decades of captivity, they had to face the daunting task of rebuilding their temple and their relationship with God. But they didn't give up. Despite opposition and setbacks, they persevered and ultimately completed the temple, rededicating it to God. This journey was not just about rebuilding a physical structure but about rebuilding their relationship with God and themselves.

The Story of Ezra

The Israelites returned to Jerusalem, but they found the city in ruins (Ezra 2:1-2). They began to rebuild the temple, but it was met with opposition from neighboring nations (Ezra 4:1-24). Under the leadership of Zerubbabel and Joshua, the people recommitted themselves to rebuilding the temple (Haggai 1:1-15). The temple was finally completed, and the people celebrated its dedication (Ezra 6:15-18).

Personal Story:

Lisa went through a tough time in her marriage a few years ago. She felt like she was at a crossroads, struggling to reconcile her desire for connection with her husband with the reality of their troubled relationship. As she began to surrender the hopelessness of her present situation and embrace the idea that God still had a future for her, she began to feel the peace of God and the contentment of her present situation. She started attending group therapy and gave God a season to work on her; while He was working on her, He was working on him, too.

Through much prayer and support and guidance from the Holy

Spirit, God was able to restore their marriage. Looking back on the experiences, as well as the refinement and brokenness, she realized that it was all worth it and that it set her up for a greater foundation for her life and her marriage.

* * *

Discussion Questions:

1. Have you ever experienced a time when God was refining you in a particular area? How did you respond, and what did you learn from the experience?

_____
_____
_____
_____
_____
_____
_____
_____
_____
_____
_____
_____
_____
_____
_____
_____
_____
_____
_____
_____
_____
_____
_____

2. How can we support each other in our own refining processes, and what are some ways we can hold each other accountable?

_____

_____

_____

_____

_____

_____

_____

_____

_____

_____

_____

_____

_____

_____

_____

3. What are some specific prayer requests we can lift up to God for one another during this time of refinement?

_____

_____

_____

_____

_____

_____

_____

_____

_____

_____

_____

_____

_____

_____

_____

Application:

Take heed to the wisdom shared below and apply the following principles to your life. Journal below to share your experiences.

1. *Reflect on your own life:* Think about areas where you've experienced brokenness or struggle. How has God been refining you in those situations?
2. *Identify resistances:* Are there specific areas where you're struggling with resistance or opposition? Pray for strength and perseverance to overcome these challenges.
3. *Rededicate yourself:* Regularly recommit yourself to God, seeking His guidance and strength for your journey.
4. *Celebrate completion:* Acknowledge the progress you've made in your spiritual journey and celebrate your increased connection with God.

_____
_____
_____
_____
_____
_____
_____
_____
_____
_____
_____
_____
_____
_____
_____
_____
_____
_____
_____

Reflection:

Reflect on the following points and journal your thoughts below.

1. *Brokenness:* Just as the temple was in ruins, our own lives can be marked by broken relationships, sin, or hurt. God uses these experiences to refine us, making us more like Christ.
2. *Resistance*: Satan and others may try to hinder our spiritual growth, just as neighboring nations opposed the Israelites. We must persevere and remain committed to God.
3. *Rededication:* Just as the Israelites recommitted themselves to rebuilding the temple, we must regularly recommit ourselves to God, seeking His guidance and strength.
4. *Completion*: The completed temple represented a new era of spiritual connection between God and His people. Similarly, when we're restored and refined through God's process, we experience a deeper connection with Him.

_____

_____

_____

_____

_____

_____

_____

_____

_____

_____

_____

_____

_____

_____

_____

_____

Prayer:

"Dear God, thank you for your promise to restore me and refine me like gold. Help me to recognize areas where I've been broken or struggled, and give me the courage to face them head-on. May I remain committed to You and trust in Your guidance as I navigate life's challenges. In Jesus' name, Amen."

Memory Verse:

"Therefore, if any man be in Christ, he is a new creature: old things are passed away; behold, all things are become new."

— 2 Corinthians 5:17 (KJV)

* * *

Take 10-15 minutes to reflect on your own refining process. What areas of your life do you feel like God is trying to refine or shape you in? What fears or doubts do you struggle with, and how do they affect your relationships with others? How have you responded to these fears and doubts in the past?

Write down three specific areas where you need to surrender your fears and doubts to God, and next to each area, write down one specific step you can take to surrender them. Commit to taking these steps and write down a specific date by which you plan to take each action.

_____

_____

_____

_____

_____

_____

_____

Week 9

Bonus Lesson: How to Study the Bible Effectively

The eyes of your understanding being enlightened; that you may know what is the hope of His calling, what are the riches of the glory of His inheritance in the saints.

— Ephesians 1:18

Objective:

By the end of this lesson, you will be able to effectively study the Bible by understanding the importance of preparation, using various study methods, and applying the Word of God to your life.

Materials include:

- Bibles
- Study materials (e.g., commentaries, concordance, maps)
- Note-taking materials (e.g., paper, pens, highlighters)

Preparation:

- Set aside dedicated time: Choose a regular time and place to study the Bible, free from distractions.
- Prepare your heart: Pray before studying, asking God to guide and illuminate your understanding.
- Understand the context: Read the passage in context by reading the surrounding verses or chapters.

Method Options:

Method 1: Observation

1. *Read the passage slowly:* Read the passage multiple times, taking note of any unfamiliar words or phrases.

2. *Identify key terms*: Highlight or underline key terms, such as names, places, and concepts.

3. *Notice structure*: Identify the structure of the passage, including paragraphs, verses, and sections.

Method 2: Interpretation

1. *Ask questions about the passage, such as:*

- Who is speaking?
- What is happening?
- Why is this important?

2. *Look for connections:* Identify connections between this passage and other parts of the Bible.

3. *Consider different views:* Explore different interpretations of the passage but remain grounded in biblical truth.

Method 3: Application

1. *Reflect on personal connections:* Consider how this passage applies to your life.

2. *Identify principles or truths:* Look for principles or truths that can be applied to your life.

3. *Make a plan:* Develop a plan to apply these principles or truths to your life.

4. Incorporate the use of additional resources:

- Use a concordance as a helpful tool for looking up specific words or phrases in different translations.
- Use commentaries to provide additional insight and explanation of difficult passages.
- Use maps and charts to help you visualize geographical and historical contexts.

5. *Take notes as you study*: This will help you remember important points and to review later.

Ways to Study the Bible:

Study Option #1:

Subject:

1. *Reading:* Read a passage or chapter that talks about forgiveness, such as Matthew 6:14-15.

2. *Studying:* Study the biblical concept of forgiveness, while looking at different passages that describe it. Ask yourself questions like:

- What does forgiveness mean in the context of my relationship with God?
- How can I apply this concept to my daily life?

3. Meditating: Reflect on how God's word has changed your understanding of forgiveness. Ask yourself how you can practice forgiveness in your daily life, and how it can bring you closer to God.

Character:

1. Reading: Read a passage or chapter that features a character like David, such as 1 Samuel 16-17.

2. Studying: Study the character of David, looking at his strengths and weaknesses. Ask yourself questions like:

- What can we learn from David's faith and trust in God?
- How can I apply his example to my own life?

3. Meditating: Reflect on how David's character can be an example for us today. Ask yourself how you can emulate his trust in God and his willingness to obey His voice.

Book:

1. Reading: Read a book like Genesis or Acts, covering the entire story from start to finish.

2. Studying: Study the book as a whole, looking at its themes, characters, and events. Ask yourself questions like:

- What is the main message of this book?
- How do the characters in this book relate to each other and to God?

3. Meditating: Reflect on how the book as a whole has impacted your understanding of God's word. Ask yourself how you can apply the lessons from this book to your daily life and how it can bring you closer to God.

Study Option #2:

Historical Context: Think of it like trying to understand a movie. You need to know when it was made, where it was set, and what was going on in the world at that time to fully understand the story. The same applies to the Bible! When we study the Bible in its historical context, we're looking at the time period, place, and culture in which the events happened. This helps us understand what the people were thinking and feeling at the time, and what the writer was trying to say.

Literary Context: Imagine reading a book or watching a movie. You can tell what kind of book it is (romance, mystery, etc.) and what the author was trying to say. The same applies to the Bible! When we study the literary context, we're looking at how the writer structured the passage, what kind of language they used, and what they were trying to convey. This helps us understand the bigger picture and what the writer was trying to say.

Cultural Context: Think of it like being a foreign exchange student in a new country. You need to learn about the customs, traditions, and values of that place to truly understand what's going on. The same applies to the Bible! When we study the cultural context, we're looking at what people believed, how they lived, and what was important to them during that time period. This helps us understand how those things might have influenced what the writer wrote and what we can learn from it.

Application: Choose a passage from your Bible that you've been wanting to study. Use the methods we've discussed to study this passage.

Reflection: Write a reflection on what you learned from this passage and how you plan to apply it to your life.

Prayer:

Dear God, Thank you for your promise to restore me and refine me like gold. Help me to recognize areas where I've been broken or struggled, and give me the courage to face them head-on. May I remain committed to you and trust in your guidance as I navigate life's challenges.

In Jesus' Name, I pray. Amen.

Broken to Build Assessment:

Are you ready to build your life God's way? This assessment is based on the book of Ezra, which focuses on rebuilding and restoring God's temple in Jerusalem.

Here are 20 questions to help you prepare for building a new foundation in life, in preparation for the induction of the new you!

1. Have you surrendered your life to God?
2. Are you willing to obey His commands?
3. Do you believe He is always with you?
4. Are you willing to forgive yourself and others?

5. Have you identified your spiritual gifts and talents?
6. Are you committed to using your gifts for God's glory?
7. Do you have a personal prayer life?
8. Are you willing to take risks for God?
9. Do you trust God's sovereignty and timing?
10. Are you willing to listen to God's voice and direction?
11. Have you let go of past hurts and regrets?
12. Are you willing to be still and wait on God?
13. Do you believe God is a God of second chances?
14. Are you willing to submit to authority and leadership?
15. Have you learned to be content in any circumstance?
16. Are you willing to be a servant-leader in your community?
17. Do you have a heart for worship and praise?
18. Are you willing to be a light in the darkness?
19. Do you believe God is capable of breaking down walls and barriers?
20. Are you willing to build relationships with others who share your values?

The Charge:

As you embark on this new chapter, remember you are not just a product of your past experiences, but a masterpiece in the making. You are a work of art crafted by the Master Artist, God Himself.

May this certificate serve as a reminder of your new identity in Christ and your commitment to living out His divine plan for your life.

The Covenant:

I, _____, do hereby declare to uphold the principles of the new me.

To live a life surrendered to God's will:

- "I have been crucified with Christ, and I no longer live, but Christ lives in me. The life I now live in the body, I live by faith in the Son of God, who loved me and gave himself for me" (Galatians 2:20).
- "Do not be conformed to the pattern of this world, but be transformed by the renewing of your mind" (Romans 12:2).
- "And we know that in all things God works for the good of those who love him, who have been called according to his purpose" (Romans 8:28).

To walk in the freedom of forgiveness and healing:

- "So, if the Son sets you free, you will be free indeed" (John 8:36).
- "He has sent me to proclaim freedom for the prisoners and recovery of sight for the blind, to set the oppressed free" (Luke 4:18).
- "Come to me, all you who are weary and burdened, and I will give you rest" (Matthew 11:28-29).

To trust in His presence and guidance:

- "And we know that in all things God works for the good of those who love him, who have been called according to his purpose" (Romans 8:28).
- "Trust in the Lord with all your heart and lean not on your own understanding; in all your ways submit to him, and he will make your paths straight" (Proverbs 3:5-6).
- "For I know the plans I have for you," declares the Lord, "plans to prosper you and not to harm you, plans to give you hope and a future" (Jeremiah 29:11).

To honor my new identity in Christ:

- "Therefore, if anyone is in Christ, he is a new creation; the old has gone, the new is here!" (2 Corinthians 5:17).
- "But because of His great love for us, God, who is rich in mercy, made us alive with Christ even when we were dead in transgressions—it is by grace you have been saved" (Ephesians 2:4-5).
- "For we are God's handiwork, created in Christ Jesus to do good works, which God prepared in advance for us to do" (Ephesians 2:10).

I vow to intentionally grow in my faith, obeying God's leading and serving others with love and compassion.

Induction into the New You:

Please accept this certificate as a symbol of your induction into the new you. May it serve as a reminder of your commitment to living out your life as a child of God, empowered by His love and guidance. Insert your name below.

_____, it is with great joy that we present to you this certificate of induction into the "New You." You are not the same person you were yesterday; you have undergone a transformative journey, and your heart has been renewed by the love and grace of God.

This certification marks the completion of your induction, as a being filled with purpose, passion, and potential. You are now empowered to live your life with confidence, hope, and courage.

Congratulations on this significant milestone!

About the Author

Crystal Love, a native of Baltimore, is a dedicated mother, Elder, and Prophet within the Christian community. She committed her life to the Lord in 1997 at the age of 17 and was called to ministry at 20. With 25 years of ministry experience, Crystal currently serves as an Elder at Kingdom Worship Center in Baltimore, MD, under the leadership of Bishop Gregory Dennis and Pastor Tonya Dennis.

Passionate about community service, Crystal volunteers in homeless shelters, teaches at women's transitional homes, engages in outreach and evangelism, and hosts empowerment events aimed at uplifting and encouraging individuals to walk in their God-given callings. In 2011, she founded Holistic Ministries, focusing on addressing the comprehensive needs of individuals—spiritual, emotional, social, and physical. Holistic Ministries, Inc. is a parachurch affiliate of Kingdom Fellowship Covenant Ministries, Inc., under the leadership of her spiritual father, Archbishop Ralph Dennis.

An author of several books that promote healing and wholeness, Crystal holds a Bachelor's degree in Pastoral Counseling, equipping her to help others recover through the power of the Holy Spirit. She is currently pursuing a Bachelor of Science degree with a focus on Religion and Christian Leadership & Ministries. Her ministry reflects her deep commitment to helping individuals discover their purpose in Jesus Christ and further expand the Kingdom of God.

"When Jesus saw him lie, and knew that he had been now a long time in that case, he saith unto him, Wilt thou be made whole?"

—John 5:6

Be sure to purchase your copy of the "Broken to Build" Bible Study Curriculum & 30-Day Devotional

For more books and updates:

🌐 crystallove-theauthor.com
✉ hello@crystallove-theauthor.com
f facebook.com/crystal_love
🐦 twitter.com/crystalcauthor
📷 instagram.com/holisticministrieslove